PARTICIPANT'S PRIMER

TEN BRAVE CHRISTIANS
THE JOHN WESLEY GREAT EXPERIMENT

DANNY MORRIS

This book is based on an earlier book titled
A Life That Really Matters.

Copyright 2012 by Danny E. Morris

All rights reserved. Written permission must be secured from the publisher to use or reproduce any part of this book, except for brief quotations in critical reviews or articles.

Unless otherwise marked, all Scripture quotations are taken from the Revised Standard Version of the Bible, copyright 1952 [2nd edition, 1971] by the Division of Christian Education of the National Council of the Churches of Christ in the United States of America. Used by permission. All rights reserved.

Printed in the United States of America

16   15   14   13   12   1   2   3   4   5

Library of Congress Control Number: 2012943464

ISBN-13: 978-1-62171-001-1

Cover design by Stephanie Wright
Page design by LeAnna Massingille

SEEDBED PUBLISHING
Sowing for a Great Awakening
204 N. Lexington Avenue, Wilmore, Kentucky 40390
www.seedbed.com

CONTENTS

PREFACE	v
INTRODUCTION	vii

PART I: PARTICIPANT INFORMATION

1. Always Fall . . . Reaching!	1
2. Unless You Want To, You Never Will	6
3. Unpacking and Using the Five Disciplines	12
4. The Witness of the People	27

PART II: LEADER INFORMATION

5. How to Begin	51
6. Presenting the Challenge	56

APPENDICES

A. Frequently Asked Questions	66
B. Commitment Form	67
C. Schedule for Morning Prayer and Scripture Reading	68
D. Scripture Readings	69

This book is based on a book originally titled *A Life That Really Matters*, which told the story of how the program, the John Wesley Great Experiment, "Wanted: Ten Brave Christians," started and what happened to the first thirty-eight people who took part in it. The spirit of the original story has carefully been retained in this retelling.

There is a separate booklet entitled *Ten Brave Christians: The John Wesley Great Experiment Participant's Notebook*. It includes journal pages for the daily half-hour devotional period.

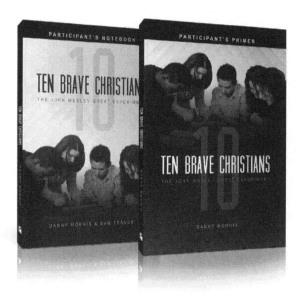

Order copies of *Ten Brave Christians: The John Wesley Great Experiment Participant's Primer* so your church can be adequately introduced to the program during your challenge period. $9.95 each

Order copies of *Ten Brave Christians: The John Wesley Great Experiment Participant's Notebook* for use by each participant. $5.95 each

See the online bookstore at www.seedbed.com.

PREFACE

During the first thirteen years of my ministry I was a witness to too few personal conversion experiences. During that time I never participated in an actual Pentecost. Until I finally did, I didn't know what I had missed.

The one who experiences a personal spiritual breakthrough thinks of it as a pinnacle moment because it is life changing. But what I didn't know is that the Christian community, itself, has a separate and unique role to play in a spiritual breakthrough. The church is a primary receptor of special visitations of the Spirit of God. A personal spiritual encounter is coveted, but when a major spiritual breakthrough is experienced by a group of people it is even more phenomenal.

God's Spirit moving upon a person blesses the church. God's Spirit moving upon a group not only blesses the church, but also empowers it for a new level of corporate spiritual vitality.

When it happens to an individual, we call it conversion. When it happens to a group, we call it Pentecost. My first Pentecost experience resulted from the John Wesley Great Experiment, "Wanted: Ten Brave Christians." I was not the prime mover; the Holy Spirit was. I did not have the leading role; Sam Teague did.

At the time, Sam was the highly dedicated, but thoroughly frustrated, teacher for our Christian Home–Builders Sunday school class. In desperation he was moved to pray for the class. He prayed for about fifteen seconds and all heaven broke loose.

Preface

The immediate visitation by the Holy Spirit within a period of twenty minutes after he prayed was a personal spiritual breakthrough that had within it the power of Pentecost. It still has that power after more than forty years.

God answered that simple prayer in a profound way. The answer was recorded. The experiment was tried. A book was written. A spiritual movement was prompted.

I was there at the time it happened in our church—first in one group, then in several. The Pentecost power broke out in spiritual vitality at John Wesley Methodist (then, not yet United Methodist) Church in Tallahassee, Florida. Since then, the challenge has spread widely and remains a remarkable ongoing catalyst for spiritual vitality.

This challenge, this great experiment, has continued to move forward for more than forty years. We no longer think of it as an "experiment," but as an invitation into an experience of the Holy Spirit.

This text contains the profound story and call that was in the original book, but is updated with a new face to the future, in the belief that the invitation needs to be sounded again.

INTRODUCTION

The challenge is frequently referred to as the Great Experiment, for it *is* a great experiment! When a person undertakes to live these disciplines it is impossible to predict the power of the Spirit's impact or the eventual outcome, and so it is a great experiment. Also, the personal interactions of the people in each group provide an experimental flavor to the process because every group is different.

In the inaugural group, we made use of five spiritual elements: prayer, service, tithing, Bible study, and Christian concern for others. What would happen when we used a catalyst—personal and total surrender to the will of God? We didn't know, and we never could have predicted what has happened.

But when one surrenders his or her life to God and practices a serious spiritual discipline, it ceases to be an "experiment" and becomes a "miracle."

How else can you describe what happens when one is "born again, not of the flesh but of the Spirit"? Even more miraculous than the blending of oil and water is the blending of the spiritual and physical into a unity dedicated, once and for all, to the will of God.

It is a miracle!

One month we were involved in a lot of nothing. The next month—through personal surrender to God and the practice of a spiritual discipline—we were involved in a miracle!

Introduction

The John Wesley Great Experiment is an appropriate name because the original challenge came to the John Wesley Methodist Church in Tallahassee, Florida.

Wesley himself was a practitioner and advocate of the serious undertaking of personal and corporate spiritual disciplines. After his famous Aldersgate experience in 1738, John Wesley discovered the genius of small groups meeting together regularly to pray, to study the Scriptures, and to witness. He found that a spiritual discipline helped prepare people to experience God's presence. He was straightforward and to the point, as are these particular challenges.

It was a spiritual discipline which was the strength of Methodism in its beginning. And it was a spiritual discipline, again in our day, that prepared the way for a breakthrough of the Holy Spirit in the life of our small congregation.

The program dimension is twofold. First, the challenge combines a variety of elements to make it a program: specific spiritual disciplines, a definite timeline, a small group culture, a particular lifestyle, a system of resources, a history, and a constituency.

Second, numerous churches have developed a pattern of presenting this challenge at specific times of the year as a part of their ongoing effort of making disciples. A church in Texas found that combining a strong emphasis on evangelism explosion methodology and offering Great Experiment groups for all new members was a winning combination for new member commitment and assimilation. It became a major part of that church's program of spiritual renewal.

"Wanted: Ten Brave Christians" is a particularly powerful phrasing of the challenge phase of interpreting the emphasis and calling for response. Think of the number of members in your church. When the invitation is expressed as a call for "ten," just ten, out of however many there are in your church, it is an ironic invitation. Out of 100 members or 540 members or 2,100 members or 4,000 members, are there even 10 who will put God first in these five simple ways for just one month?

When the invitation is initially considered, one may quickly conclude that ten out of this many will be as easy as a snap of fingers.

"Wanted: Ten Brave Christians!" Are there ten who will put God first in their lives in these specific ways? The real question, when viewed from a personal standpoint, isn't "are there ten?" but "will I be one?" This straightforward, disarming challenge has a way of becoming very personal. "If I am so sure we will find ten, why have I not decided to participate?"

Over a period of four to six weeks this challenge was earnestly presented through a series of sermons interpreting the five disciplines. Sunday school class interpretations and discussions augmented the teaching quality during this period. Such a period in any church, devoted to presenting the challenge, will not be time wasted.

In the month of March, twenty-two persons in our church tried this spiritual discipline and it changed their lives. In April, another sixteen persons tried it and their lives were changed. It changed the life of our church. It changed the life of the minister of the church. We know it works!

I am confident that it is God's plan for us to have a life that matters. Such a life can be built only as we are truly committed to doing God's will.

PART I: PARTICIPANT INFORMATION

Chapter One

ALWAYS FALL . . . REACHING!

"Always fall . . . reaching" must have been the motto of countless persons across the centuries. If one falls while reaching, he or she is more concerned about reaching than about falling, or with protecting oneself in the fall. To fall while reaching is to hold on to your goal, even while falling; it is to be concerned with someone or something bigger than yourself. It connotes a remarkable disposition and effort, including sacrifice when needed.

Sam Teague was a father of five, a banker, mayor of Florida's capital city, later elected state senator, a highly regarded speaker in his own church and other churches, who, on the morning of January 24, 1965, must have felt like he was falling. He was unaccustomed to the feeling.

He had lots of good things going for him, but on that morning he would not have included on that list our Christian Home–Builders Sunday school class, of which he was the teacher. He knew that it was not going well, though the class members probably thought it was. They knew they were fortunate to have Sam as their teacher. The class was delighted, even if Sam was discouraged. They were giving their teacher an enthusiastic "hearing" each Sunday, but he felt that their response was less than it should be.

For Sam, listening to the gospel and actually *hearing* it were not the same. They listened, but they didn't hear. That difference resulted in the frustration he was feeling on that Sunday morning. He had occasionally talked with me about how disappointed he was that even though his class members were bright, well educated, and stimulating, something was missing. For a long time he couldn't put his finger on it. Finally, it became clear to him. What was missing was their fervent response to the gospel.

When he would vent his frustrations to me, my plan was always the same. I would hear him out, affirm his assessment, and encourage him to "go back into the game and give it your best." After all, teachers like Sam were hard to find.

His custom on Sunday was to go very early to his office in the bank and finalize his presentation for the class by preparing himself in a time of prayer and silence. Since arriving at his office at about 6:50 on January 24, he had prayed, sat in silence for a while, and then had begun to concentrate on the simple survey he had asked his students to answer the previous Sunday: "Write the ten things that you want out of life in order of importance."

After tabulating thirty-three responses, he was shocked. The five or six most popular choices were simply things, material possessions: a new car, a second car, a house, a cottage at the coast, a boat, a different boat, financial security, money for vacation.

At long last he had found a key: *They think the purpose of their lives is to be happy, and they think that the acquisition of things will make them happy.* The shutter clicked and the picture was clear. Sam knew one can never find happiness by setting out to be happy. He knew that happiness is a byproduct, not an end in itself.

Jesus never talked about being happy. He was pretty strong and absolutely clear on "taking up your cross," wearing "My yoke," going the second mile, giving to the poor, "dying and rising with Me." None of this is happiness language. But when life is lived like this, happiness comes and is transformed into joy, and joy is real!

Later that morning, Sam planned to tell his class about the results of the survey and had made a note to ask: Why do you think you have a right to be happy? The purpose of your life is not to be happy, but for your life to matter. If you set out to find happiness by itself, you will never find it. If you have a life that matters, happiness will come.

After reviewing his teaching notes, he looked at the clock—9:00, time to go. He placed his notes into his briefcase and snapped it closed, but before standing he looked off into the distance and reflected on the deeper implications of his discovery. With most of them under age thirty-five, he realized that with their current attitudes, they would have a lifetime of unhappiness even while desperately pursuing happiness.

He thought, *Why am I doing this? What's the use? Nothing seems to get through to them. With so much potential, they are like plastic people in their understanding of the gospel.* For weeks Sam had conducted a series about some of Jesus' strong words. He felt the class had no clue as to what Jesus meant when he said, "You are light . . . You are salt . . . You are a city set upon a hill. Take My yoke upon you . . ." They didn't understand the power of these words.

Although he felt himself falling into utter frustration, he began reaching that morning. Reaching to God! Reaching to his students.

He leaned forward in his chair and put his head on the desk. He reached out with a brief, but desperate prayer, "O God, show me how to challenge these young people so they can have a life that matters!"

It was a prayer, but there was no time for an "Amen." Instantly, a thought came to Sam and he reached for a manila pad. A second thought almost overlapped the first. The ideas, thoughts, and concepts began to flow. He wrote rapidly, trying to capture everything. He flipped one page, then another. The avalanche of ideas continued.

The pace of his breathing increased as he began to sense a presence in the room. Although he was locked inside the bank, and his office door was closed, Sam felt he was no longer alone. There was a Presence! At one point, he actually turned to see if someone was standing behind him.

Looking back to the page, he had the sense that something was being written through his hand. It was a strange feeling, like he was not really connected to what was happening, but yet it was being done through him. Strange, but not frightening.

Sam kept rapidly writing and flipping page after page. Finally, it stopped. It ended and there was nothing more to write. It was over. No more thoughts and ideas. No more Presence.

With a deep exhale, Sam looked at the clock. It was 9:20. After praying a fifteen-second prayer, it had taken him twenty minutes to write God's answer. In that twenty minutes he had written the challenge of the Great Experiment, "Wanted: Ten Brave Christians," just as it had been given to him. This would be an experiment of "putting God first" for one month. Much more was written, but this was the heart of the challenge.

He quickly read over the pages he had scribbled and put in a few plainly lettered words where they were needed. Sam then drove to the church and proceeded as he had planned, but he didn't mention anything about the prayer or what had followed it. He did say in two or three different ways that the purpose of life is not to be happy, but to have a life that matters.

The Christian Home–Builders class was stunned. Their cages had been rattled. A popular misconception had been challenged. As the class ended, the members were speechless.

On the way home, Sam recalled the name of the class and thought, *This morning we may have turned a corner in understanding how to build Christian homes. It has to do with putting God first in your life to the best of your ability, every day, in every way.*

Chapter Two

UNLESS YOU WANT TO, YOU NEVER WILL

Sam and I had been friends for a dozen years, fishing and hunting partners for several. After starting the John Wesley Methodist Church together five years before, we had grown even closer. I frequently stopped by his office for coffee and conversation.

On the Monday morning following his fifteen-second prayer, we were awaiting delivery of our breakfast in the coffee shop next door to his office. Sam handed me a sheet of paper and said, "Take a look at this and tell me what you think."

I read,

Wanted: Ten Brave Christians who, for one month, will put God first in the following ways:

1. Meet once a week to learn how to pray.
2. Work at least two hours in the church each week and do a daily good deed.
3. Give God one-tenth of your earnings.
4. Spend from 5:30 to 6:00 each morning in prayer and the study of Scripture.
5. Witness about your experience with God to others.

My response was, "Where did you get this?"

"I'll tell you later. What do you think about it?"

I read the paper again.

"You aren't planning to do this in our church, are you?"

He kept pressing, "Tell me what you think."

As I took a deep breath I felt the blood leave my face. I realized I was severely threatened by what I was reading. We sat in silence until long after our breakfast came. I really appreciated the silence and I was glad Sam didn't press me further. I had all I could deal with in my sense of threat at that moment.

You see, I was the only pastor that church had ever had. I not only knew all of the nearly four hundred members, I knew them well. When I looked at those five challenges and thought about the people of our church, I was suddenly confronted with how weak and thin my spiritual leadership had been. My thing in the church was being optimistic, cheerful, fun loving—not spiritual. This challenge was deeply spiritual.

My feeling of threat was so great that I felt like striking out. I wanted to ask, "Do you think that many of our members will actually work in the church for two hours each week for a month?" I didn't ask the question because a hint of anger didn't seem appropriate right then. My anger had come quickly because of the fact that for a long time I had found it easier to do things myself than to try to talk half-interested people into doing something, and then have to complete what they had half-done, or clean up their mess after them. I had given up thinking it could ever be any other way. I had become cynical and weary. The emphasis on prayer, tithing, Bible study, doing something for someone else out of love—none of these had ever been my "thing" to preach about, to call for, or to expect.

I was becoming more and more uncomfortable. My feeling of being threatened went even deeper when I looked at the number "ten." I thought, *I am the only pastor this church has ever had. If we can't find* ten *out of more than four hundred who will do this, how will it make me look?* It felt like a brick had hit my stomach.

It was at about this point that the Holy Spirit began to minister to me. After looking up, and then back at the paper Sam had handed me, I began to think not of how our church was, but how it was intended to be! I remembered reading something Albert Einstein said, "The church in Germany was eventually the only force that stood squarely across Hitler's path to suppress the truth." (But we were not that kind of church!) Victor Hugo said, "The church is the anvil that has worn out many hammers." (But that was not us!)

I also thought of some things Jesus said, and immediately I realized that in a mystical way He could have been talking about our church: "You are the salt of the earth;" "You are the light of the world;" "You are My body in the world." That is us! That may not be what we were right then, but that is what we are supposed to be—the body of Christ! For the first time, I wanted that to be true of our church. I felt courage growing in me, and I leaned forward to say, "Let's see if we can find ten who will do these five things! If we can, it will blow the lid off our church. And if we can't, I will have something to preach about the rest of my life!"

That breakfast meeting was on January 25, 1965. Through the month of February we presented a robust challenge to "put God first" in our lives. On March 1, we began the experiment. There were twenty-two in the prayer group in March and sixteen more in April. Christ began to change people, empower them, set them free, heal, give new life, and fill them with love. These things happened to almost everyone in the two groups and to some who were not in a group. After February and March of 1965, John Wesley Methodist Church was never the same again!

When the Christian Home–Builders class began considering this concept of putting God first, it was almost beyond their grasp. But after two or three sessions they began to understand that the teachings of modern-day culture and society had misled them.

They began to think seriously that perhaps the purpose of life is not necessarily to be happy, but to build a life that matters, and began to ask, "How do I build such a life?"

Sam felt that persons could never build a life that matters unless they came to love God with all their heart and all their mind and all their soul and all their strength. But how to get the class members to grasp this was a difficult undertaking! Never in their entire lives had they been asked to truly surrender their lives to Christ.

During the first several class sessions there was reluctance for them to even talk about "surrendering your lives to God." Nearly everyone felt that to surrender would require doing something strange, mysterious, and unusual. Sam did not lessen the fears. Rather, he told them that not one of them could know the great power that God could release in their lives until they first, "sought Him with all their hearts." One way to do this was through the Great Experiment.

The class was told that this program would especially welcome those who were discouraged and had nowhere else to turn, those who were afraid and had nowhere else to hide, those who were disappointed after having tried everything else, those who were lonely and wanted once again (or for the first time) to feel the great surge of God's love and power in their lives.

By this time, most of the class members had begun to realize that building "a life that matters" would require a substantial effort on their part. Realization came that everyone would be faced with a decision; some would decide to try and build a life that matters, and others would decide to be content with their lives as they were.

The class lessons began to bear down hard on the "how" of building a life that matters. Sunday after Sunday the class was challenged to face up to what really matters in life. This confrontation began to have a profound effect upon the attitude of the majority of the Christian Home–Builders class.

On the fifth Sunday, Sam opened the lesson by saying, "You are just wasting your time unless you are ready to surrender your life to God totally. You must be ready to practice (1) self-surrender, (2) self-denial, (3) self-discipline, and (4) self-sacrifice."

He then called for a response, hoping that there would be at least ten members of the class who would be willing to give their lives to God totally for one month. There was no question in Sam's mind that if a small group would let God take over their lives for one month, it would cause a spiritual revolution within the church.

The lid *did* blow off our church. The twenty-two in March and sixteen in April who responded began to walk into deep water and to experience the fire of the Spirit. Water and fire are appropriate metaphors—*water* of baptism, cleansing and refreshment. *Fire* of the Holy Spirit within them and in the challenges they were called to.

Unless you want to
Put God First,
you never will!

Unless you want to
Live the Disciplined Spiritual Life,
you never will!

Unless you want to
Experiment with the Christian Faith,
you never will!

Unless you want to
Understand the Joy of Giving,
you never will!

Unless you want to
Release the Power of Committed Laity,
you never will!

Unless you want to
Experience the Strength of Small Groups of People Walking a Stretch with Each Other,
you never will!

Unless you want to
Discover the Power of Corporate Spiritual Discipline,
you never will!

Chapter Three

UNPACKING AND USING THE FIVE DISCIPLINES

"Wanted: Ten Brave Christians" is an irony-laden, piercing probe that cannot be easily ignored by the congregation.

After a substantial effort to challenge the congregation by using "Wanted: Ten Brave Christians" as the flag of choice, let there be a response Sunday followed by a reasonable window of opportunity for persons to respond. The week following the response Sunday and the next Sunday will be ample time to gather the final responses and commence the groups.

When the groups begin, two adjustments are absolutely necessary: First, drop the terminology "Wanted: Ten Brave Christians." It should be dropped because the challenge has served its purpose. Those who are ready have responded. Those who did not respond should not be badgered.

Another reason to drop it is that no inference should be made that those who have responded have, thereby, become "Brave Christians." No terminology or label should suggest they have. One does not become a "Brave Christian" by joining one of these groups. That designation is only for one who makes a total surrender to God. What God asks of a person can never be done alone; only God can see him or her through. It is one's faith response in obedience and God working through the person that makes one a "Brave Christian."

Second, all of the groups immediately go underground. Within the church, hopefully, the challenge has been spirited, and the invitation has been open and clear. The matter has been thoroughly discussed for quite awhile. When the groups begin, the congregation will welcome a change of subject.

Underground groups are also best because what occurs is kept within the groups through a strong code of confidentiality. Absolutely no effort is made to whet the latent interest of persons who did not respond.

After the groups begin, they are to be referred to as "Great Experiment Groups."

Several important factors make a good weekly meeting. Give due consideration to these elements.

1. Focus on prayer and learning to pray.
2. Share with one another how the week has gone.
3. Have devotional Bible study and purposeful discussion.
4. Hold all meetings at the same place each week. Do not serve refreshments.
5. Have the same convenor/guide for the month.
6. Remain focused on the subject of "putting God first."
7. Have several inspirational books on the table at each meeting and invite everyone to read or peruse a book each week.
8. Stress the urgency of confidentiality. A good rule of thumb is that anyone may tell outside the group anything that happened to oneself, but should never tell outside the group what happened to another member.

We turn now to an inside look at the five disciplines. There are subtle rhythms even in the numbered order of the disciplines. The first discipline is on prayer—an inward experience. The second is on service in the church—an outward experience. Tithing is an inward experience that is outwardly expressed. Silence, journaling, and studying Scripture focuses on the day. How to build and develop your life focuses on the future.

This rhythm, therefore, becomes a positive spiritual cross-current within the small group setting. For all of its simplicity, the dynamics are present for the Great Experiment to make a dramatic impact upon the participants, and through them, upon the church and the world. When a church has multiple groups at the same time, and new groups are regularly being formed, the groups become a hotbed of spiritual ferment within the church. Let us unpack each of the five disciplines to discover their uniqueness.

Discipline One
Meet Once a Week to Learn How to Pray

"Can I really learn how to pray?" is a common question for many people. Though closely held and not often asked in public, the question can be haunting.

The first discipline in the Great Experiment offers an emphatic "yes" to that question. That answer becomes a conclusive and convincing, "Yes, you can learn how to pray!"

The following are components of the weekly group meeting:

I. The First Half Hour Is for Talking about Prayer and Actually Praying.

The weekly hour-and-a-half group meeting is specifically devoted to learning how to pray (and to two other important matters). About one-third of the time is spent in talking about prayer and praying.

In the first month of our Great Experiment group we discovered it is important to put the half hour for prayer at the beginning of the meeting. Often the enthusiasm of the meeting will crowd out or use up the time allocated for the meeting and cause prayer to be curtailed. Prayer is too important to be left until last or to be shortchanged in its allotted time.

1. There is teaching and discussion about how to pray and a variety of types of prayer experiences are featured.
2. Within the group, requests for prayer are freely called for and answers to prayer are carefully recorded.
3. Initially, persons are invited to pray silently. Later, the invitation will be given to pray voluntarily a sentence prayer. No one is ever forced to pray or to pray in a way that makes him/her feel uncomfortable.
4. The spirit and practices of prayer are positive and contagious.
5. Simple invitations and directions for prayer are varied.
   - *Call for two minutes of silent prayer followed by the Lord's Prayer in unison. (Across the month, the time for silence may be lengthened.)*
   - *Invite anyone to say aloud a single word that expresses how one feels at the moment. (This is a simple form of prayer.)*
   - *Offer a prayer-word of thanksgiving to God.*
   - *Use a prayer-song, which the group may sing together.*
6. Invite persons to talk about meaningful times of prayer in their past, during the past week, or today.
7. Associate these half-hour prayer-labs with the need for and possibilities of prayer in the coming week.
8. Suggest simple ways to pray in the coming week.

Although only one-third of the weekly meeting is about prayer and learning how to pray, the entire hour-and-a-half meeting has the quality of a prayer group meeting.

II. The Second Half Hour Is for Talking about How the Other Disciplines Went during the Past Week.
1. How have you done with the two hours of working in the church and doing a daily good deed?
   Ask members to be specific. Encourage them to not get behind in their schedule of service in and through the church. Expect

reports of success and failures. Ask for stories about daily good deeds. This can be a rich time of realism, humor, honesty, confession, new resolves, etc.
2. What have you learned about tithing?
How is it going? How do you feel about it? What are you learning about the use of your money? What are you learning about your relationship to God?
3. How have you done with witnessing?
Many people have lots of confusion about witnessing. Simply put, witnessing is freely telling someone about something that happened to you. How to do that with grace and in good taste is a subject that can be helpful to a group of beginners. Within the group we discovered that witnessing is the most natural and comfortable thing a person does when something good has happened, and he/she is eager to tell someone about it. We also discovered that the reason some of us had negative feelings about witnessing was that nothing especially good was happening or we had been negatively conditioned about witnessing, so we felt we had nothing to talk about.

III. The Third Half Hour Is for Reflecting on the Daily Scripture Passages.

Each morning at 5:30, the assigned passage of Scripture of no more than nine verses is read, prayed about, and reflected upon in writing. The third half hour of the group meeting focuses on the passages from the past week. It is a rich time of getting into the Word and getting the Word into the group, which may be very different from reflecting upon it alone.

It is Bible study, but the goal is not to do biblical criticism, nor is it a time for testing a person's orthodoxy. The purpose is to share the Scripture, devotionally. Ideally, all seven passages that were read during the week are reviewed. Questions, comments, interpretations of meaning, and increased familiarity with Scripture are goals of this phase of the meeting.

Many people leave a Great Experiment group meeting with comments like: "Where have these passages been all of my life?" Or, "I didn't know that was in the Bible." Or, "The Bible is something else, isn't it?"

Discipline Two
Work At Least Two Hours in the Church Each Week and Do a Daily Good Deed

"Unless we can do it in the spirit of love . . ."

As a pastor, I have experienced many major discoveries about my sense of frustration and burnout. One discovery was that being a workaholic was not fulfilling. But I found it easier to do it myself than to try to find others who would commit to a project and follow through to its completion. At the time our Great Experiment started, I often felt like a basket case with everything I had to do. It caused anger in me. I had lived with it for so long, I no longer knew the source of those negative feelings.

When the Great Experiment started, I discovered for the first time the power of a highly motivated and spiritually committed laity. In March we had twenty-two people who were doing 2 hours of service in the church each week for a total of 44 hours a week or 176 hours within the month. They continued serving 2 hours during the next month and were joined by sixteen more people. By the end of April we had had 480 hours of work done in the church by both groups. By the middle of the first month my attitude had changed, and so had my problem!

My problem now was that we had run out of things for people to do. I didn't know what to suggest for them to do because I couldn't just give them "busy work." They were serious about living out their faith and the work had to have meaning. By the middle of March we were beginning to run out of things to do. All of the prospects and shut-ins had been visited; people in the hospitals were being systematically visited by our laity for the first time; the flower beds were in great shape; the choir was full; we had one Sunday school teacher for every eight children; and the classrooms had been painted.

And my attitude: within far less than two months I found new hope for the church. Those dry bones were alive for the first time.

Our laity's eagerness to respond was carefully honored and managed. At the first meeting of the month we presented a list of things that needed to be done in the life of the church. Here is the list we prepared:

A Beginning List

Please read over this beginning list of opportunities for service and choose the items that will challenge you most.

1. Visit hospital patients or shut-ins, representing the church.
2. Visit present members to tell them about your experience in the Great Experiment.
3. Visit families interested in our church and invite them to join. (Names will be provided by the church secretary.)
4. Be a teacher or helper in a Sunday school class for a month. (Count one hour for preparation as helper and one hour for class time.)
5. Join the choir for a month. (Count as one hour per week.)
6. Visit in your neighborhood for one or two hours to find "prospects" for the church. Invite them and report prospects to the pastor.
7. Within your neighborhood, spend an hour visiting two or three church families whom you do not know in order to get acquainted and to talk about our church and its needs—spiritual and physical.

8. Visit with some new members to get acquainted, to welcome them, to tell them of your experience. Perhaps two or three can be visited in an hour. (The pastor will furnish names.)
9. Help provide Sunday school room improvements. (The trustees will guide you.)
10. Make contact by telephone (one hour per week) with persons who "need" a call. (Names will be provided through the church office.)
11. Work out details for, and promote the formation of a church library during the month.
12. Work in the church office (one or two hours).
13. Work on the church grounds (a continuing need).
14. Contact visitors from the previous Sunday in their homes.
15. Use your imagination to discover other things the church needs you to do.

We asked everyone to select an item and put his or her name by it so needed coordination could be done, so overlaps could be spotted, and so gaps could be filled. These were accountability sheets, not for reprimanding anyone, but to underscore the urgency of the commitment. The list also reflected the strength of our corporate efforts.

We encouraged everyone to strive to put in their two hours week-by-week instead of saving up for one big day of service at the end of the month. One can fulfill the "letter of the commitment" that way, but the spirit of ongoing service to God would be missed.

There is no way to overstate the spiritual and physical revolution within our church experienced through this simple discipline of a few people working at least two hours in the church each week.

Because of the response of these persons, I no longer had reasons for negative feelings. They became self-starters, initiators, and innovators. I was shocked at the change from one month to the next.

As a church we had made two of our greatest discoveries: (1) everything that is done in the church must be done in the spirit of love and (2) the church needs nothing done in its life that cannot be done in the spirit of love—nothing!

During my first morning devotional of the program, I had an epiphany when confronted with the task of praying about choosing one good deed for the day. The contrast provided by focusing on God and His Holy Word in the first ten minutes, then focusing on my own heart, dying to self, and becoming more Christlike through helping others was very revealing. I did okay with the first ten minutes and was able to move right into the scriptural "oughtness" for that day. But when I moved on to the second ten minutes and selecting a "good deed," I ran out of time because ten minutes was not enough. Since we had been told of the value of disciplining ourselves not to tarry, but to move on in the pattern of the three ten-minute segments—it being so early in the morning with the natural tendency to be overcome with sleepiness—I moved beyond the second ten minutes to the exercise of the final ten minutes. I planned to later return to my effort to decide on a good deed. When I finished and returned to the second ten-minute exercise, I continued to be stumped on naming a good deed.

Every good deed I thought of would not hold up under the guidelines that had been suggested: "Select a good deed you will not get paid to do or you are not obligated to do." Visiting someone in the hospital might qualify as a legitimate good deed for others but not for me. I was getting paid and was obligated to visit people in the hospital.

Even—and maybe especially—Brother Tom "paid" me when he would say, "Danny, seeing you just makes my day and gives me such a lift." Pretty good pay for a brief visit! No one else told me that. Hearing something like that made it worthwhile to go out to the hospital. I began to evaluate my motive for the things I was doing—"for others."

On the previous day I would have honestly said that maybe 75 to 80 percent of my deeds for others were done unselfishly. But consider this: Why did it eventually take me one hour and forty minutes that day to think of one unselfish thing I could do for just one person in an entire day?

I was at first chagrined and then devastated by how self-centered and self-serving I was. (I will explain more about this revelation under the discussion of Discipline Four.)

Discipline Three
Give God One-Tenth of Your Earnings

"Giving until it helps" became a goal of our church.

It was surprising to me to learn that the challenge of tithing for a month was one of the disciplines of the Great Experiment. I had not learned much from being a tither for more than a dozen years, so I wondered what could be learned about tithing in just a month.

The reason I had been tithing all of my adult life was that I knew I was supposed to promote tithing and, therefore, I needed to be doing it if I expected others to do it.

I had tithed all that time and hated every minute of it! I had missed the significance of tithing in two ways: (1) I had a poor motivation for doing it and (2) I had done it the wrong way.

When Sam began advocating tithing in his class he suggested a different way of doing it.

First, he made it clear that the reason for tithing was to put God first. I had never understood that before. I saw tithing as an official requirement of my job as a pastor, which made it feel like legalism.

Second, he invited (taught) us to take the tithe out first: "Let your tithe be the first check you write when you get paid. Put God first in spending your money."

What he said seemed so right.

I had been doing exactly the opposite of what he was suggesting; I had always given my tithe last, after everything else had been paid—and when I was about to, or had already, run out of money. I was doing it legalistically, so I put it off as long as I could, and ended up giving begrudgingly most of the time. It was a continuing chore because I was ignoring the instruction that each one should give "not reluctantly or under compulsion, for God loves a cheerful giver" (2 Cor. 9:7).

But in the Great Experiment, we were taught to give our tithe first. This was a tangible way we could begin to practice putting God first.

What a difference even one month of tithing this way made for my wife, Rosalie, and me. Tithing suddenly became a joy and a religious experience. It became that way because we were now putting God first in the very important matter of our money.

The third thing Sam suggested was that we pray about how we spend the other nine-tenths. Rosalie and I had never prayed about how we spent our money. The closest we had come was praying because we needed more money. If taking the tithe out first sounded right, praying about how we spent the other nine-tenths sounded absolutely necessary. We were struggling to live off of ten-tenths and sometimes eleven-tenths or twelve-tenths. How could we manage on only nine-tenths? Prayer was absolutely necessary!

Remember, some of the things we regularly talked about at our weekly meetings were prayer, tithing, how it was going with us, etc. As we talked in our group, we discovered we were all "in the same boat." Before we began tithing, none of us felt that even ten-tenths was enough for our needs.

But as the stories began to accumulate, we heard over and over that since beginning to tithe in these ways, money seemed to go further. Nine-tenths became as much or more than ten-tenths had been. The difference was not because anyone received a raise, nor because there was magic in prayer. Rather, we discovered there was power in prayer. Money had now become a spiritual matter. It became supremely important that we spend our money prayerfully. That helped us to spend it more wisely.

Discipline Four
Spend from 5:30 to 6:00 Each Morning in Prayer and the Study of Scripture

Where has the Bible been all of my life?

The early morning time of prayer and meditation quickly gave rise to this question. That half hour is a powerful part of this challenge. One reason is the uniqueness of three ten-minute segments of the devotional period.

In the first ten minutes, you read a different passage of Scripture each day, pray about its meaning, and write in less than fifty words what the passage says to you.

During the second ten minutes, you pray about one good deed you will do for someone that day and record the details of your plan in your notebook.

The final ten minutes are reserved for determining how you want to build and develop your life and then putting the plan in writing.

After eventually finishing the three segments, I was just sitting there. I noticed that both of my elbows were resting on the arms of my chair. It seemed a natural alignment to cause my fists to rest against each other, knuckles touching. I began to rotate one fist one way and one the other. This simple action dramatized the disharmony I had discovered about myself. How it "ought" to be, and how it "really was" with me were not in sync. That was a tough discovery.

With this shattering image of disharmony in my life before me, I reconsidered what I had written earlier when I had jumped ahead to the assignment for the third ten minutes. I read my answer to the question, "How do you want to build and develop your life?" I could now see it clearly. What I had written earlier was pitiful, flimsy, shallow, and out of focus.

I put my fists back together, knuckles touching, and rotated them again as before to be reminded of the disharmony within my life. Suddenly, there was no mystery about why I was feeling that my life was not together, why I was feeling fractured. I was out of sync with God's plan for me. The evidence was right there in the out-of-focus statement I had just written about building and developing my life.

I began rotating my fists back and forth again, but this time I did it with my wrists turning together in the same direction. That was a distinct picture of the harmony I wanted in my life. I could see clearly what was needed. Now I could really answer the question, "How do you want to build and develop your life?" (Just one thought per day will be excellent progress.) That question now had meaning. I scratched through what I had just written, so I could write something new. But I didn't stop with just one thought. I wrote and wrote in my daily journal as insights flooded my mind. This dynamic rhythm of God's oughtness, my response (reflected in struggling with the good deed), and insight about building and developing my life, had walloped me the very first day. I was not the only one who would experience this powerful purging.

On about the third day in our group a man answered the question about building and developing his life: "I want to be a millionaire!" he said. He was already well on his way to attaining his goal. Toward the end of the month he wrote in the margin of that page: "This goal is not good enough for a child of God!" Another evidence that the Holy Spirit was moving in us.

Observations about the three ten-minute practices of meditation:

- This is a powerful, but simple structure for a devotional period.

- It is simple enough for the beginner and challenging enough to be beneficial for anyone.

- It serves as a reality check for everyone who will stand in the crosscurrents of these three movements for thirty (or thirty-one) days.

- To top it off, the person meets weekly for discussion—for confirmation or confession—with others who are doing the same devotional discipline.

- This half-hour, early morning, daily devotional period is a remarkable experience.

Discipline Five
Witness About Your Experience with God to Others

What is so wonderful about a Christian witness? And what is so frightening about it?

Of all the disciplines, witnessing was probably the most challenging. Some would even say it was the most frightening. A few people later said they decided not to participate in the Great Experiment because of the call to witness. Previously they had been turned off by stereotypes of people standing on the street corner passing out tracts, or by street preachers, or by having been accosted by someone about religion.

That was not the type of witnessing being advocated. We talked a lot about how natural witnessing is and how simply it can be done. Many examples came forth as a result of our willingness to experiment with witnessing. Some of our efforts were successful and some were not. We learned from each other, and we practiced witnessing within the group by telling each other when something that was being said or done was negative or did not communicate.

All of the persons who participated committed themselves to "Witness for God your experience to others." The members of the group found it a joy to tell of how God was working in their lives.

Someone put it like this: "Yes, the rich experiences of this month of spiritual discipline must be shared. We must share our experiences so anyone who wants God in his life will know at least one way of opening his life for God to come in."

Chapter Four

THE WITNESS OF THE PEOPLE

There are many factors that make a Christian witness powerful and one of the most essential forms of communication the church has ever produced:

simplicity	the truth it reveals
authenticity	mystery
clarity	surprise
passion	necessity
the story it tells	

In short, there is nothing that can take the place of a vital and alive personal Christian witness. The church thrives on it and is strengthened and thrilled by it. The church is hungry for it and wants to hear it, to foster it, and to ensure that it continues. When someone gives her Christian witness, either in what she says or in what she does, it produces gladness, goodness, and hope to all who hear it or see it.

When we began to take personal witnessing seriously in our group, everyone was timid and cautious. We had seldom (or never) witnessed and we were unsure, or even fearful.

Our group read what R. L. Johnson of Albany, Georgia, said about witnessing in his personal testimony.

I will challenge any man or woman to sit quietly in prayer and meditation at 5:30 AM for thirty days, and then tell me that he prays but his prayers have no meaning.

I will challenge any man or woman to plan a totally unexpected and unselfish deed daily for thirty days, and then tell me she does not love her fellow man.

I will challenge any man or woman to set to writing bit by bit over a period of thirty days at 5:30 AM what he expects to make of his life, and then tell me he has made no effort to conform to the written design.

I will challenge anyone to perform the three above functions, and then say he or she does not enjoy sharing his experience with others.

Here are five examples from among many that illustrate some of the values of witnessing which we began to discover in our group. These seem to fit naturally within the five disciplines of the Great Experiment.

Discipline One in Practice
MEET ONCE A WEEK TO LEARN HOW TO PRAY

Here I Go Again
Elizabeth DuBois Russo

In March of 1985, I was finishing the last semester of law school at Washington University in St. Louis, about to turn thirty, experiencing crises in my personal life, and physically run-down. I was at a major crossroad. I was receiving counseling from a very good therapist, and trying to stay with an aerobics program. I also went to church on Sundays.

But something was terribly wrong. I always felt that God was in my life, but something was missing.

I had been hearing about the John Wesley Great Experiment that our church was going to be conducting during the month of March. It sounded intriguing: "Wanted: Ten Brave Christians." Although I'm sometimes lazy about mundane things, if you put Mt. Everest in front of me I say, "Let's go!" This sounded like a challenge.

What finally hooked me was a young mother about my age witnessing from the pulpit one morning. She spoke intelligently and passionately about being a strong-willed woman who was working hard for success and wanting a strong family life and a life that matters. She spoke of learning how to put God first in her life and how it wasn't easy, but she spoke of many gifts given to her in return.

After the worship service, I attended a brief but serious meeting outlining the expectations of undertaking this program. I felt like I was joining the Marines or signing on to be a monk in the fourteenth century, but it struck me as something I had to do.

Over the weeks that followed, I struggled with the issue of prayer. I felt that I had always talked to God, but that it was my own little secret. The prayers that I had grown up knowing I tended to mumble thoughtlessly, with my mind turned elsewhere. And those prayers would only be heard on Sundays or at the dinner table (occasionally) or sometimes at night when I felt my daughter should be brought up right. But I wasn't listening and I wasn't really opening myself up for communication. And while I at first thought of many reasons why I shouldn't have to get up at 5:30 in the morning and pray on my knees and really think about it, I had committed to do these very things and I was determined.

The changes in my life during and after those weeks were subtle, yet profound. I was still struggling, but I had the most powerful tool one could have—the power of prayer. Through prayer and the communion with people I met in my group (there were twelve of us), I learned to really examine my life and give it meaningful direction. I reacquainted myself with the notion of thinking and caring for others and added a new twist (for me)—doing things for them without expectation of thanks or recognition.

Best of all, I have learned to really open myself up to talking to God, and when words fail me, to say, "Show me the way, Lord," and then listen. The answer always comes. Sometimes, I had to be told or shown many times before I got it, but I always felt the gift of peace that comes with knowing that sooner or later the answer will come.

I was excited about re-upping again thirteen years later. I have spoken many times of how this Great Experiment has changed my life, and was excited that my church in Connecticut was willing to undertake it in 1998.

Discipline Two in Practice
WORK AT LEAST TWO HOURS IN THE CHURCH EACH WEEK AND DO A DAILY GOOD DEED

Spiritual Growth at Maggie Jones Memorial United Methodist Church
John Hitz

How the Holy Spirit began to move among us!
In March of 1995, I promised to help the chairperson of our spiritual formation committee introduce the John Wesley Great Experiment program to a nearby church (since I had participated in the program every March since 1990). I briefly explained the experiment and the seed was planted. Nine people responded. The Great Experiment was the kindled ember that was needed within this body of Christ.

Our weekly prayer time in the group became a bonded nucleus within the church and the emphasis which was needed to ignite the remainder of the church family. As the month came to a close, two very significant events took place.

The first was a workday for the "two hours of work each week." While a contractor was painting the outside of the church, some members of the congregation painted the inside—those who were participating in the group and some who were not. The church had not been painted in fourteen years. Later in the month, the curtains were washed and ironed. Others cleaned windows, cleaned and organized shelves, several of the men installed two iron railings at a side entrance, pews were polished, floors were swept and mopped, the carpet was vacuumed, and food and drinks were prepared for our lunch and snack times. Without at first realizing what was happening, this small rural church was receiving the empowerment of the Holy Spirit, and everyone felt that each was being conformed into the image of Christ for others.

The other event that occurred during the John Wesley Great Experiment took place the last Monday in March. I had also been participating with a Great Experiment group at my home church, Maggie Jones UMC. Both churches had exchanged names with each other for prayer, but they only knew each other as a name on a piece of paper. I proposed to each group that on the last Monday in the month we all meet as a combined group at Maggie Jones Church. It would be a time for prayer, for sharing experiences that had occurred during the month, and for fellowship between the two churches. The Holy Spirit blessed each person who attended that evening.

As the year progressed, there were several events which denoted new life and enthusiasm as the Holy Spirit continued to move us and move in us at Maggie Jones UMC:

1. A new roof was put on the church after fifteen years.
2. Special music during the worship service began to be more frequent.
3. A Bible study group was begun on Sunday evenings by the lay leader of the church.
4. Attendance at Sunday worship began to increase, and eventually, nearly doubled.
5. Another Bible study group was begun on Wednesday mornings for the women of the church.
6. The idea of discernment and consensus was reintroduced for our church conference.
7. All churches in the community were invited to a New Year's Eve service, a potluck dinner, and Eucharist. Three youth were baptized that evening.
8. I completed requirements to become a part-time pastor and was appointed to Maggie Jones Memorial Church.

How the Holy Spirit moves!

Discipline Three in Practice
GIVE GOD ONE-TENTH OF YOUR EARNINGS

My Story
John E. "Jack" Turner

When the Ten Brave Christians challenge was first presented at John Wesley Church in the spring of 1965, it appealed to me—except the part about tithing. Because of unusual financial demands at that time, I decided to pass on it. But when Danny made the call on the following Sunday, I went to the altar and made a commitment that I have never regretted.

The Ten Brave Christians disciplines made me look at myself as I had never done before, and I did not like what I saw.

It literally turned my life around. I, of course, tithed for that month and have done so, and more, ever since. Tithing is just a part of our lives. We give off of the top and never stop to ask, "Can we afford it?" It has never been hard for us, even though our income has been meager compared to today's incomes since our retirement in 1977. Money has never been a problem. As one of our former pastors, Tom Farmer, would say, "Thank you, Jesus."

I have gone through the Ten Brave Christians program twice since 1965, and I have been renewed and blessed each time, but nothing like that original month in 1965. It was truly a spiritual awakening like nothing I have ever experienced. I will always be grateful. It has helped me to be a better Christian in all that I have done since. Thanks be to God!

Discipline Four in Practice
SPEND FROM 5:30 TO 6:00 EACH MORNING IN PRAYER AND THE STUDY OF SCRIPTURE

Meeting with God, Daily
James Goode

Following a lay witness mission at Palm Springs (U)MC, Hialeah, Florida, in September 1971, my wife, Katherine ("Kat"), and I wanted to become disciples of Jesus Christ. We were joined by eight others in a prayer group. We were using the book *A Life That Really Matters* [now *Ten Brave Christians: The John Wesley Great Experiment*] by Danny Morris.

After a few days into this Ten Brave Christians program, our pastor, Bill Swygert, invited Danny (who was serving as pastor of a nearby church) to bring a few laypersons from his church who had gone through this course to meet with our group. Danny shared some insights and thoughts with us for a few minutes before introducing our other guests and offering us the opportunity to ask questions.

I knew that Kat was struggling with getting up for Bible study at 5:30 AM. She didn't understand why she could not just get up "an hour earlier than usual." We had three young children who placed a lot of demands on her time and energy. Since she was a little shy, I asked about this for her. Danny called on an elderly woman to share her experience about the early morning prayer time.

She said that at first she had struggled with the same problem, but God revealed to her that she had an appointment with Him (along with nine other people in her group) at 5:30 AM. That answer helped Kat to realize the importance of meeting with God daily at a specific time. After that realization, Kat never had a problem with getting up at 5:30 AM to meet with God. Almost twenty-six years later, she continues to meet with God for an hour or more in the very early morning.

Discipline Five in Practice
WITNESS ABOUT YOUR EXPERIENCE WITH GOD TO OTHERS

The Mayor
Sam Teague as told to Danny Morris

As mayor of Tallahassee, Sam and other city officials had struggled over a pesky problem that no one had solved: how to keep a dependable night janitor for the new airport. There were many complaints about the dirty terminal. Several attempts had failed, and the little problem remained unsolved for so long, it had become a "big" problem. However, the man who was currently employed had been doing a good job for several months.

Sam was making a 6:15 flight to Atlanta and decided to go to the airport early enough to have a visit with this worker. Because of the relative smallness of the airport, the mayor went walking about and found the man mopping the floor in one end of the terminal. He walked up and told him his name, shook hands with him, and said, "I am the mayor and I want to thank you for the good job you are doing. I thank you on behalf of all of our citizens."

The janitor just stood there without saying a word.

Again Sam shook his hand and called him by name, saying, "Thank you, Mr. ———."

Tears were welling up in the fellow's eyes. He was finally able to get his words out.

"Thank you. I can't remember when anyone has told me I am doing a good job."

That was a powerful and unforgettable moment for the janitor and for Sam. And it was the same for our group. We had just heard the story of a Christian witness, which came right up out of Sam's life situation, out of who he was and what needed to be done.

So this is what a Christian witness is! There was nothing scary about that. It was natural. A little effort was required, but the result was worth the effort. We began to feel that any of us could do "something like that." No tracts were passed out, no Bible was thumped or shaken in anyone's face. No accusing finger of judgment was pointed. No one had been embarrassed. All in all, it had been a good experience for both of them. One person had communicated to another person a sense of caring, concern, and appreciation. None of us doubted that Christ was present in that early morning meeting.

The mid-sixties were exciting years! Space exploration was just getting started. *Sputnick* was launched. John Glenn orbited the earth and walked on the moon. Space travel was inaugurated—big time.

The Space Program became a metaphor for what was happening in our Great Experiment groups. As our participants *experimented* with five biblical, authentic, orthodox spiritual practices, many were being "launched into orbit." What was happening was phenomenal! None of us had ever experienced anything like it. We were doing more than undertaking spiritual disciplines—which in itself was amazingly significant—discovering the power of small groups for the first time, and finding spiritual vitality. Many of our people experienced profound *spiritual* callings and had the sense of being "launched into *spiritual* orbit!"

CALLINGS

Called to New Birth Through Prayer
Danny Morris

About a week before I assisted with Merle Jackson's funeral, she wrote me a long letter reviewing her story she had shared with me. Early on in the letter she stated that she didn't know how her story would be beneficial to anyone else, but she was glad to share it if it might.

She recounted a spring afternoon about twenty-eight years ago. She and her husband were sitting on the patio. Suddenly, she looked at her watch, jumped up, and hurried away saying, "Jack, don't worry about me, I am going to the church." She described how panicked she felt when she realized that the first Great Experiment group in our church was starting at 7:00 PM. The time had slipped up on her; it was already 7:10. She drove wildly, by her own description. Once parked, she ran to the front of the church and suddenly froze in her steps.

She looked at the flowerpot beside the steps and the clump of daffodils that were "blooming their hearts out," as she put it. She had never before noticed the flowerpot, but *she had seen those daffodils*—in a wonderful dream two nights before. There was no doubt; it was the same bunch of daffodils. She stood absolutely still trying to put together her dream, the flowers which she was seeing now for the second time, and her utter excitement of finally being at the church—even if a little late.

She wrote about that moment:

> I hesitated in the narthex because I could hear you speaking to the group. The meeting had already begun. My heart sank. How could I walk in late? But I had to do it! I took a deep breath and pushed open the door. You looked my way and said, "Oh, Merle. We've been waiting for you. Welcome home!" And I timidly entered and sat down.
>
> Danny, I knew that you had spoken those words and that you were just being hospitable. But to me, it was as if those words were spoken to me by God: *Merle, we've been waiting for you. Welcome home!* As I sat down, tears were flowing down my face. I sat there trembling, weeping, *coming home*, feeling for the first time that God really loved me! I listened to everything you said that day with a great sense of awe. I couldn't wait for the first day to begin our Great Experiment. Oh! It was *something*! Prayer . . . the group . . . discussing Scripture . . . talking about

our good deeds each day . . . laughing a lot—and all the while, being spiritually born anew. I mean, *totally, new birth*!

Danny, I am in my early seventies, but my life actually began only twenty-eight years ago when we had our first Great Experiment group at the church. Do you understand what I am saying? That is when my life began. I was *born* just twenty-eight years ago!

As I read her letter, I thought about the telephone call I received from Merle on my birthday more than twenty years ago. She always sent me a birthday card, with a poem she had written, and usually a letter. But when she called that day she gave me the greatest birthday gift I have ever received. She briefly reviewed these facts of her journey and said, "Danny, you led me into a totally new life, in Christ. I began to live for the first time while you were here. You will never know what you mean to me."

Her generous accolades made me feel uncomfortable, so I interrupted by saying, "Thank you, Merle. It is so kind of you to say those things."

Then came her gift to me. She said, "Danny, there has never been a day since Christ came into my life that I have failed to pray for you by name. I have never missed a day praying for you!"

I was stunned!

I said, "Merle . . . I am so moved to hear you say that! My word . . . what a gift to give me on my birthday—the greatest gift I could ever receive. Merle . . . thank you!"

When I got near the end of her letter, written just a week before she died, she said again, "Danny, I have prayed for you by name every day since I was converted twenty-eight years ago."

In the Great Experiment, the first thing Merle committed to do was to "learn how to pray." I was the beneficiary of her prayers. As I have reflected on her gift, I have concluded that Merle's faithfulness in prayer and her continuing love for me have been shaping influences upon my life and ministry.

As we flew to Florida for her funeral, I thought about how fortunate I was to have been the one Merle selected to pray for by name every day. At her funeral, I told about her call on my birthday and what it had meant to me across the years. I could not keep back my tears as I spoke about it.

After the service, four people came to me and said that Merle had also prayed for them every day by name for years! I wondered how many more there are whose names she regularly called in prayer.

When the fourth person came to me to say that Merle had prayed for her, I said, "Isn't that just like her? And all this time I thought I was special!" We laughed, and my friend said, "All of us were special to Merle."

I think it is fair to say that no matter what else she got out of the Great Experiment, Merle learned how to pray!

Called to Love
Joanne Surles

I had been looking for something all my life, but I looked in all the wrong places. Although I was brought up in the church, I never seemed to reach anything spiritual there. As I grew older, church became a social thing. About the only time I was ever touched in church was by an occasional favorite old song. But even then the good feeling I received was just a short-lived emotion.

As I grew older, I became guilt ridden as I did things I had been taught not to do, but because I could think of no "valid" reason not to do them, I continued to live as I pleased. In doing so I became nervous, irritable, and cynical. I began having headaches, an upset stomach (the beginning of an ulcer), and many other aches and pains too numerous to mention.

I would sometimes sit up in bed in the middle of the night in a cold sweat, wondering what was to become of me. I prayed, but never really expected my prayers to be answered, and they never were! I talked to probably a half-dozen ministers and psychologists. They listened patiently to my complaints, told me I should mature, sympathized with me in all my trials and tribulations, and showed me the door. Each time I left as confused and cynical as when I arrived.

Then I heard about the Ten Brave Christians experiment at Sunday school. I felt an immediate urge to try it, but because all my friends were anything but spiritually minded, I knew they would tease me. I also felt I would never be able to pray in public or witness to others. I have always been mortally afraid to speak a word in front of a group.

To my surprise, my husband expected from the beginning that I would join the group. He said, "If this can change your life, you'll be able to witness." On the last day before the program started, I decided as a last resort to put everything I had into the Great Experiment.

By the third morning, during my 5:30 session, I prayed as I had never prayed before. I brought up honestly all the sins that I had tried to hide from myself for years; all the guilt, all the fears, all the worries.

The next morning I went to the church, ostensibly to do my two hours' work, but really to talk to the pastor. I poured out to him my doubts, and he helped me to begin to understand how juvenile my ideas were about God. That afternoon, I had what I felt was a completely new and original idea: *God is love!* That concept was so new to me that I was overwhelmed! God was not in the clouds, or next door, or with the preacher: God was in my heart and God's love was flowing over me like waves in the ocean! How could I ever explain my joy on that day?

I had found a reason for living! I had found a peace I had never thought was possible. The wonder and joy I felt were so immense that words could not express it! I felt God's love pouring through my body and pulsing through my veins. I loved everybody and I wanted to tell them of my discovery.

As I went about my tasks the follwng day, the answers to all the questions I had been worrying about for years came pouring into my consciousness so rapidly I simply could not digest them all at once.

I felt that if I could only turn my eyes inward, I would be able to see God face-to-face. I had such a strong feeling of God's presence that I actually looked in the mirror and was surprised to see that I had not changed at all.

I don't expect to have an experience like that again until I die. In fact, that day I thought, *This is what heaven will be like, only more so.* And I still believe this to be true.

I am learning more about God's plan for me. Every day is an adventure, as exciting as it was when I was a child.

When I give myself to God's direction, it is unbelievable how smoothly the day runs. Even the little things, such as finding parking places, finding people in when I call, and many other little incidents seem to click into place. When I am about to do something that is not God's will, I feel an uncomfortable twinge and there is no doubt in my mind that I should not do it.

When I look back and realize how my life has been changed, I can hardly believe it. I came away from this experience with a sense of complete dedication and trust in God. I am not able to keep my faith pure, and sometimes I am very discouraged with myself for straying from what I know I should do. I feel so humble when I realize that anything I do for God is less than an atom when compared with what God has done for me.

Called to Ministry
J. Michael Waldrop

I was a management consultant for a United States firm consulting in Asia. My wife, Becky, and I had just returned from living overseas. Exciting as it was, life there had been a very difficult and dry time for both of us spiritually. Then came the Great Experiment, "Wanted: Ten Brave Christians." We knew we had to be involved and were drawn in by a shared feeling of urgency. We were expecting to go back to Hong Kong after a couple of years of living stateside while our son, Jonathan, finished high school. We wanted to be better prepared spiritually for life far from home, family, and the spiritual support of a congregation. The opportunity for participating in a small group and for a renewed prayer life were exactly the things we had been looking for.

The results of our participation in the Great Experiment are impossible to describe in a few words. Something unbelievable began to happen to the members of our group as we prayed. Not only were our prayers answered, not only did God use each of us to affect loving changes in others, but feelings of love and power began to surround us all. We were opening up, taking risks, reaching out in new, courageous ways. We were beginning, slowly and fearfully at first, to surrender ourselves to the God who made us and knows us and loves us beyond our understanding. It would be a life's work to appropriate the full meaning of this discovery, but we had made a beginning together. We had several Great Experiment groups going on at once in our church. The wind of the Spirit began to blow through the entire church—binding, healing, and challenging.

In just those short thirty days, God made it possible for me to renew and heal my relationship with my father. It seemed to be a key that unlocked my own capacity for love. It was a new freedom; it was life renewing. Now I was capable of a more compassionate, loving relationship, opening myself to others . . . to intimacy . . . to God.

When the thirty days were over, there were so many miracles in our group, all of us became convinced of the power of prayer. When the group discussed continuing, we were led to meet monthly for the next two years. The Ten Brave Christians program was the beginning of our intense journey toward a more committed life of discipleship.

It was the group that served as a "Clearness Committee" when Becky and I sought clarity in my answering God's call to ordained ministry. It seems that we did not need to prepare for a return trip to Asia after all. We had found a whole new life instead—a life of ministry in Christ.

Becky and I introduced the Great Experiment at my first appointment as an associate pastor. We recognized an intense hunger for spiritual growth in the congregation, very much like what we had felt. What we had experienced through the Holy Spirit began to work in the church to change lives as they, too, discovered the power of prayer and practiced the five disciplines for thirty days. To date, more than seventy members have begun this journey of spiritual growth in our church. Some of the covenant groups are still meeting. Many have become the newly empowered leaders in our congregation—answering God's call on their lives and discovering new identities in Christ Jesus.

We have come to believe that there is a great hunger in the church and in the world for a deeper experience of God. We know of no better starting place for those just beginning their journey of faith, and no better place for renewal for those further along on the journey, than the Great Experiment. *These thirty days could change your life.*

Called to a New Kind of Church
Becky Waldrop

It was a bad time in our church—a time of conflict and dissatisfaction—a time of changes long overdue. We all showed up at the administrative board meetings fully prepared—each of us with our own *Book of Discipline* held firmly in our laps, sure of our positions, holding those who were a bit less sure in contempt, and arguing with pharisaical glee. We made sure our alliances were secure and our points well made. The board meetings were the best attended in years.

While we were feeling the heavy responsibilities of running the church and beginning to be a little alarmed at how mean other people could become at our board meetings, someone was beginning something called the John Wesley Great Experiment. The newsletter article said, "Wanted: Ten Brave Christians!" It was right next to the yearly announcement that the United Methodist Women (UMW) were planning their fall bazaar.

This year the UMW's project was more important than usual. There had been a noticeable decline in the giving of our congregation and an ensuing financial crunch. Someone had the idea that it would be nice if all the women would work together to make a single quilt to auction off at the bazaar. It would be a "big ticket" item and seemed easy enough to do if everyone helped. A few of the real quilters made little kits of fabric and instructions for those less experienced to assemble into individual squares. These would be returned and pieced together to construct the quilt.

I was not active in the UMW and, not being a quilter, I was somewhat concerned as to how I would put the pieces together—but I took four little bags of gold and brown calico pieces home with me anyway. I also did something even more risky than that—I decided I would begin the John Wesley Great Experiment when it started the following month.

I worked and worked on those four quilt squares in the interim. The instructions were great, but no matter how I tried, I could *not* get the squares to work out the same size as the pattern called for. I even took one apart and reassembled it, but it was no use. I felt really badly about it and wondered whether they could even use my eccentric little squares that wouldn't measure out right and looked a little worn and frayed from my feverish efforts. But I took them back to church (not knowing what else to do with them) and gave them to my friends with profuse apologies. They just smiled at me and showed me a lot of other squares they had received. Some were even a worse mess than mine—more like triangles than squares! Some had the different colors in all the wrong places. Some seemed to be coming apart at the seams already. I went away feeling very sorry for whoever might attempt to put all those defective squares together. I was certain that there would be no quilt at the bazaar.

As for the John Wesley Great Experiment, I began to feel somewhat less "brave" about participating in the upcoming program than I had before. Maybe I really was too busy with the problems of the church right now to be out yet another night of the week praying.

I missed the bazaar itself, but was surprised to hear that one of the women of the church bought the quilt. I finally had the chance to see it when it had been spread on the altar in a special Thanksgiving weekend arrangement. Spilling out across it were all the fruits of the harvest, a cornucopia of plenty, a riotous celebration of God's faithfulness and grace. And, in the center, sitting atop our many calico squares, was the chalice and a loaf of fresh bread.

Quite suddenly the image of that patchwork table pierced my "Let's all make nice, its Sunday" consciousness and seemed to explode inside me. I wanted to stand up and shout: "Look! A miracle! Can't you see it?" For our squares were all together. It was a quilt and it was beautiful!

As the communion liturgy began and I watched our congregation file down, one-by-one to dip their bread into the same cup, I mentally deposited my *Book of Discipline* back in its spot on the shelf. For here, finally, was the church. Here was the body of Christ—all of us, without exception, as eccentric and broken as those funny, shabby little squares in our quilt. And here was the quilt—mysteriously and wondrously sewn together with loving hands.

I sat through the whole service with tears on my cheeks. It no longer mattered now which squares were mine, for I was a part of something new and suddenly achingly real to me—a community of faith. Perhaps others saw it, too—I don't know. No one stood up and shouted that day. . . . But soon after that we began to lose interest in our tiny power struggles.

The Great Experiment had finally begun and for thirty days we were doing it for real. We were learning to pray . . . some of us for the first time in our lives. We prayed for each other. We prayed for ourselves. We prayed for our church, and a wind began to blow through its buildings. Changes were made and a community of God's people stood up, and began, at first timidly, and then gradually more boldly to bring all those pieces of themselves and place them in very loving and very powerful hands. Amen.

Called to a New Life
Ben C. Johnson

For three months, I had heard of the work of the Holy Spirit that was underway at the John Wesley Church. How I wanted to talk with these folks who had been in the stream of the Spirit! Danny Morris, whom I had recently met, filled me with expectancy.

Finally, a time came when I could visit. One by one, I listened to living witnesses of Jesus Christ.

As others were sharing, I kept noticing out of the corner of my eye a slightly built man sitting two seats from me. All the time the others were talking he kept switching from hip to hip as though he could not sit still. He smiled . . . he twisted his hands . . . he looked at the group . . . and twisted some more! Like a three-year-old at Churchill Downs on Derby Day, he kept standing in the shoot ready to run. I wondered what he had to say.

Finally, the man who couldn't sit still got his turn. His name was "Happy" Woodham. He began, "This is the greatest thing in the world, this brave Christian deal." As he talked, his countenance glowed with mingled joy, love, and excitement. He was contagious!

"I will tell you what this spiritual discipline has done for me"—all the time he was switching hips, twisting his hands, and making a few amusing faces—"it has changed my life."

He went on to tell about several things that had long been deep problems for him, and his recent victory over them. Happy's own joyous, jovial spirit would have been witness enough; his worded expression added something else. Then he said, "You know, the Lord has a sense of humor too," and he related this experience.

> The other night while I was having my evening prayer time, I really made contact, got plugged in . . .

you know! It was a wonderful time. But when I finished and crawled into bed, I got scared nearly to death. The room had been completely dark for quite awhile. I casually opened my eyes and began to see lights flashing on and off. One here, one there. Everywhere I looked there were little lights all in the room flashing on and off . . . on and off!

I sat up in bed and whispered to my wife, "Rose, Rose, wake up! Rose, wake up, I'm about to have a vision." I hadn't been a Christian but three months and here I was having a vision already!

Then Rose sat up. She looked about, hopeful to share in my vision. For an instant she, too, was stunned by what she saw.

I whispered, "I don't know anything about visions! Can you make out any meaning to it?"

Then Rose exclaimed, "Happy, you aren't having a vision . . . those are lightning bugs that got out of little Peggy's fruit jar!"

I agree with Happy, "The Lord does have a sense of humor!"

A Retrospective
Thomas E. Farmer Jr.

In June of 1972, when I was appointed pastor of John Wesley (U)MC in Tallahassee, Florida, the most amazing thing I discovered upon arrival was the absence of the Ten Brave Christians program. I had heard of the dynamic impact of this month-long discipline of practicing the basics of our faith and had looked forward to being the pastor of the church where God birthed this opportunity for spiritual renewal through Sam Teague and former pastor of John Wesley UMC, Danny Morris. Much to my dismay and surprise, I found that the experiment in discipleship had been dormant in the church for several years.

When some friends and colleagues found out about my appointment to John Wesley, they joked and jived, "Oh yeah—that's where you can find ten brave Christians, if you're lucky!" Or, on a kinder note, some would ask, "Isn't that the church where the Ten Brave Christian movement started?" Still others said, "Let me know what happened to the ten brave followers of Jesus!"

Upon arrival I did just that—I found them! As a matter of fact, what I found was that although the experiment was no longer being emphasized by their pastor, the men and women who were in the initial groups with Sam and Danny were still among the remnant of faithful, sincere, and accountable members of the Lord's Church! Yes, the Ten Brave Christians were still there—tithing, praying, loving God, and serving His church!

On the first Sunday in July 1972, I invited those who would like to, to join me in a month of the Ten Brave Christians program. Much to my heart's delight, the altar filled with faithful folk who were hungry for more of God,

Jesus, and the Holy Spirit! Twenty-two persons came forward at the close of the service. That was exactly the number that was in the first group in 1965.

Since that day, I have utilized the Great Experiment in every church I have served as pastor—and with the same results: cleansing, renewal, revival, restoration, and deepening of the lives of the persons who dare to put God first for one month!

There will always be suspicious scoffers along the sidelines when any serious attempt at spiritual renewal is made. The sad thing is that these persons usually stay right there on the sidelines, never taking up for themselves the challenge made by our Lord to "follow Me." And it is even sadder that they never find the joy that awaits an accountable surrender to the Lord and deepening of the walk of faith.

For twenty-six years I have offered the Ten Brave Christians program to the three congregations that I have served, and literally hundreds of lives have been greatly blessed and dozens have been eternally changed by participating in this Great Experiment. I have yet to find one person who stayed with the program for the entire month that has anything but praise and thanksgiving to God for having participated.

PART II: LEADER INFORMATION

Chapter Five

HOW TO BEGIN

Begin with the pastor who longs for the members of the congregation to respond to a unique spiritual challenge. This is not to imply that the church has seldom or never been spiritually challenged. But it is to say that presenting the challenge of the Great Experiment—"Wanted: Ten Brave Christians"—will accomplish several worthwhile goals:

1. **It is a short-term challenge.** Ideally the church-wide period of challenge is presented over a four- to six-week period. The invitation is to participate in the group for one month, although many groups choose to continue longer than a month.
2. **The disciplines are spiritual dynamite.** They appear to be simple—and they are—but in their uniqueness and simplicity they have great spiritual power. They set forth biblical foundations for beginning the spiritual life. Changes that come to persons are often for a lifetime, and many people continue practicing the disciplines.
3. **The Great Experiment is comprehensive.** The disciplines are not all that the church is about, but when they are practiced together, they provide great spiritual power. Consider the varied challenges they present: learning to pray, serving in the church, tithing, praying and meditating on Scripture, meeting with a small group, doing a daily good deed, and building and developing your life.

4. **It is exceedingly personal.** You deal with your own "stuff" within your life situation. You decide how far you want to go and how deep. You choose what you want to talk about in your group. You decide on the commitments you wish to make. Within the group, everyone is praying daily for you by name. This fact alone can open windows of wonder. Group members begin to expect and recognize miracles in each other's lives. In our hearts we intend to support the church with our prayers, our presence, our gifts, and our service. All these commitments are actualized through this challenge.
5. **It is powerfully corporate.** There is great strength in corporate discipline. Here, you are not pushed along, but supported forward by the efforts of others who are also putting God first. You begin to see your own strengths and weaknesses more clearly as you move along with others who are trying to stand tall, but sometimes stumble. You learn a lot about yourself.
6. **It is a lifetime opportunity.** When you make the choice to put God first, you will have a lifetime not to regret it, but—on the contrary—to make the most of it.

Begin with a layperson who will say, "Come on, Pastor, let's get serious about our relationship with God in Christ and how we love and serve people. We want to open up the Bible and let it speak to our deepest needs so our lives can be spiritually formed in Christ. Let our church specialize in making Christian disciples and sending them forth into the world. Teach us how to pray. Call us to deeper spiritual commitment."

Somebody needs to feel a hunger for a spiritually transformed life. That is a beginning. If no one feels that hunger, perhaps no one wants to change.

Realistically, we must face the fact that not every person who tries the Great Experiment will have a dramatically transformed life. The reason: not every person will finally surrender his or her life to God through Christ in a given month. And without complete and total surrender, God cannot completely transform a life.

If you were to become a member of such a group and your group experienced about the same response as other groups, this is what you might look forward to:

- One-third of your group would have transformed lives.
- One-third would be deeply affected, and along with the first one-third, would want to continue.
- The remaining one-third would not be too deeply affected.

Of the first two-thirds of your group, all that needs to be said is that they will have found the secret to having a life that matters, and if they continue to put God first in their lives and love God with all of their heart, all of their mind, and all of their strength, they will never go back to their old way of living.

Of the last one-third to whom nothing happened, we now know that if they will try and try again (with special emphasis on learning how to pray), some of them will sooner or later surrender their lives to God and discover a new life. A common characteristic of this latter one-third is that they are waiting for something to happen—waiting for God to bring about a sudden miracle in their lives. Generally, it does not come this way. When it does come, it will be the result of some specific effort on their part to become aware of God and serve God by the surrender of their lives to God's will.

Throughout the challenge period, make frequent announcements designating the day when the group(s) will start. Repeat over and over the specifics of getting the group(s) underway. Describe the various ways persons may make a response. Make it clear that you will be calling for a decision "to put God first" in specific ways for thirty days—just to see what will happen.

Be cheerful as you present the challenge. These spiritual disciplines are not legalisms, demands, or even requests. They are invitations to grace through grace. Do not present the challenge harshly or with the slightest hint of anxiety or pressure. You extend the invitation; God does the calling.

The goal is that just about everyone who wants to will have read this book before the month begins. Reading all about the challenge is important because there is far more to it than one will discover just by reading the five disciplines. A good understanding makes long friendships, and understanding all that is involved here makes good Great Experiment groups. The more persons who read and understand the challenge, the better will be the response.

Toward the last of the period of preparation, the Commitment Form on page 67 should be copied and made available upon request to all who are interested. There are always some whose decision is fleeting. The best procedure is to ask the interested person to take the form home, pray about it, fill it out, and mail it to the person in your group who is selected to receive the written commitments. Not everyone will follow through. But those who do follow through with the commitment in this way are really interested, and their desire and/or sense of need makes a difference.

The "Schedule for Morning Prayer and Scripture Reading" on page 68 and the Scripture readings for the month on page 69 should be copied and made available to each participant.

A notebook for keeping a spiritual diary will become a treasure to each participant. The *Ten Brave Christians: The John Wesley Great Experiment Participant's Notebook* is available for this purpose.

Finally, this fact must be faced: There is absolutely no substitute for concerned and consecrated laypersons who want for themselves and their church a life that really matters. Let them come forward and join with their pastor in presenting the challenge to a deeper commitment in Christ.

Let the pastor join with them in sounding the uncompromised gospel call to Christian commitment. This emphasis cannot be delegated as a responsibility. There must be at least one person—lay or clergy—who will put God first in his or her life and lovingly, patiently, and prayerfully invite others to do the same.

After the preaching and teaching period there comes the experiment. This invitation is not just to form a unique new group, or to do something spiritual, but to put God first, and that is a serious matter.

Chapter Six

PRESENTING THE CHALLENGE

Ten Brave Christians is a significant spiritual formation challenge for a congregation and it should be handled accordingly. It is a bold challenge to put God first in our lives through authentic and powerful spiritual disciplines. Many people have said that these disciplines are like spiritual dynamite. We would not handle actual dynamite carelessly, and we must not handle spiritual dynamite with any less caution.

Your church will benefit by successively focusing on one of the disciplines each Sunday. Then, on the sixth Sunday, invite persons to respond to be in a Great Experiment group. Interpret each discipline carefully so all can determine if they wish to participate in a group that will experiment with the disciplines.

Consider each of the spiritual disciplines on its own merit. As you present successive points of the challenge each Sunday, people will begin to view them cumulatively. Each is strong in itself, but when they are practiced together, they build strength like matches do when several are tied together with a string.

Order enough copies of *Ten Brave Christians: The John Wesley Great Experiment* to accommodate the size of your congregation. During the interpretation and challenge period ask people to check out a book to read about how the Great Experiment started, the details of the challenge, and what some participants have said about it. Ask everyone who checks out a book to read it within two or three days and return it so others can check it out. Encourage as many as possible to read the book during the six-week challenge and interpretation period.

TO THE PASTOR(S)

Do not try to jump-start a group. The result is seldom worth the effort when . . .

1. persons enter into this challenge without understanding the implications of putting God first.
2. they are enthusiastic but poorly informed.
3. they become caught up in the moment by hearing someone else's enthusiasm or persuasion.
4. they decide to do it because someone they like or admire is doing it.
5. they respond impetuously on the spur of the moment.

There is little reason to hope that a jump-start will be a meaningful experience—much less a life-changing one.

Also, do not try to handpick a group of friends, church leaders, or persons you know who *need* this challenge. The result will likely backfire and the effort can become divisive.

Go church-wide with the challenge. Present it boldly. Teach it. Preach it. Aim for the greatest response that is possible. A five-Sunday series on the disciplines is a good way to present the challenge. Although the challenge can be presented more briefly, there is much preaching and teaching content within the five disciplines.

On the First Sunday
Preach about learning how to pray.

Talk about prayer in your own life, about great persons of prayer you have known, about how this prayer group will work, what it will be like to be in a group, what such groups can mean to the church, and other "calls to prayer." Assure everyone that they will learn about prayer and how to pray, but they will *not* be manipulated, embarrassed, or forced to pray, or have to pray aloud.

On the Second Sunday
Preach about service to God and to people.

Working at least two hours in the church each week is usually not a major threat. Two hours is not a long time, but it will be impressive if you multiply it out and show what an impact will be made by ten people who work two hours a week for four weeks. What if you had five, or ten, or twelve such groups—and additional groups in subsequent months?

Present your adapted list of things the church needs people to do based on the example provided on pages 18–19. Suggest that each person will be asked to select how they will work in the church two hours each week and keep up with their commitment each week.

Preach on *diakonia* (service) and *koinonia* (fellowship). They are like two sides of the same coin.

On the Third Sunday
Preach and teach on tithing.

Tithing has been a major emphasis in the entirety of Judeo-Christian history and tradition. It is not well understood, and is actually misunderstood, by many of our people.

The Great Experiment is an experiment in Christian tithing. Talk about practical aspects of tithing: How to figure the tithe—on gross or net income? Is one tithing while contributing to the upkeep of an elderly parent? What guidance can you give when the person in the group wants to tithe for the month and their mate does not want to? How can a non-employed spouse participate when he or she earns no direct income, but feels a call or a desire to tithe?

Any of these considerations are powerful prompts to the pastor in giving guidance that is theologically sound, practical, and helpful.

There are two additional dimensions of tithing which need to be clearly annunciated:

1. Take the tithe out first.
2. Pray about how you spend the other nine-tenths.

These are amazing rubrics that have wonderful theological and practical gifts for the persons who actually practice them.

After the third Sunday, announce the Commitment Sunday and the "Come and See" meeting. (They will be detailed later.)

On the Fourth Sunday
Preach and teach about prayer, Bible study, and how you want to build and develop your life.

Make this a Sunday that everyone will remember.

Give details of the pattern of using the first ten minutes of the devotional perod for studying and writing about a Scripture passage; the second ten minutes to pray about and write a good deed you will do for someone that day; and the third ten minutes to write at least one thought per day about how you would like to build and develop your life.

Many will not have had experience with a devotional period, especially at 5:30 in the morning. As you make practical suggestions, they will see how simple the practice is and they will be encouraged to do it.

Also encourage your people to learn how to study the Bible devotionally, how to care for others, and how to put God first!

Continue to announce the Commitment Sunday and the "Come and See" meeting.

On the Fifth Sunday
Speak on witnessing.

For many people, witnessing will be the most frightening part of the challenge. As you present this part of the challenge, be enthusiastic and cheerful, even humorous. This attitude will help to relieve anxiety about this subject.

Also, define Christian witnessing. A simple definition: We witness only about what we have seen, or what we have heard, or what we have experienced and know to be true. Illustrate with examples of persons they know who have a Christian witness, by telling of your experience of witnessing, and by naming some places or situations where a Christian witness is needed. Help them see that witnessing is as natural as breathing—once we have something to witness about.

Remind them that the group will provide a little "laboratory" for experimenting with witnessing, and encouraging everyone to try it.

Announce the "Come and See" meeting again.

The Sixth Sunday
Commitment Sunday

Commitment Sunday is the day everyone has been anticipating. Make it an upbeat and lively service. Review all of the parts of the challenge, emphasizing the high points. Include the youth! Call for a response, utilizing one or more of the following options:

1. Invite persons to come forward and stand together as a group at the altar or chancel. (Sometimes, someone will be encouraged to respond when they see a particular person come forward.)

2. Invite persons to fill out the registration slip in the bulletin and put it in the offering plate or in a basket placed for the purpose.
3. Invite persons to mail in their commitment to join the group prior to _____ (set a final date after the following Sunday). This will allow a week and two Sundays for people to respond.

Announce the ultimate deadline for making the commitment to be in the group. Example: The deadline is defined by the mailed envelope being "postmarked by midnight" on Tuesday night after the seventh Sunday. That becomes the deadline for responding to be in the group. No one will be in the group who responds after the deadline.

This group is officially closed at the designated time. Later respondents will be asked to wait for the beginning of the next group.

The "Come and See" Meeting

Once one or all three options to respond have been offered, and people have responded, announce a "Come and See" meeting to close the preaching/teaching series. This is like casting the final net! The meeting should last no more than an hour. It is necessary because several weeks have been devoted to presenting the challenge, and some interested persons may have been absent one or more Sundays. At the meeting, present the total challenge in a brief and clear review and invite the persons who wish to participate to kneel at the chancel or altar for their prayer of commitment. Provide a three-by-five card for them to sign and note their selected times for the weekly group meeting.

The "Come and See" meeting should be announced for the week following the first Commitment Sunday. There are four ways to respond:
1. Come forward within the group on the sixth Sunday.
2. Deposit one's commitment in church.

3. Mail in the commitment.
4. Kneel at the altar for prayer, and select the time to meet from among the options offered.

This meeting is to be attended by every youth and adult who is considering—or has decided—to be in a group. Announce leaders, locations, and the time for the meetings. Some of those attending the meeting will have already decided; others will not be sure. It is often helpful for everyone to hear about the entire challenge in one sitting. For any who missed a Sunday or so, such a review is often an encouragement to make a decision to participate.

Give a final invitation to respond by asking them to fill out their card, take it to the altar or designated place, and pray a prayer of commitment before they leave. The simple card should list their name, contact information, and their choice of the time/group they plan to attend.

In the meeting, try to accomplish the following:

1. Adequately publicize the name of group leaders, and where and when the groups will meet.
2. Give ample opportunity for persons to respond: the "Come and See" meeting, Sunday school classes, the deadline to mail in commitment forms, or to notify the pastor.
3. Close the group for the month as of the final time for commitment. (Everyone needs to begin together.)
4. Ensure that all groups "go underground" and that the code of confidentiality is strictly observed.
5. Announce all Great Experiment group meetings in the bulletin and newsletter, but do not "beat the drum" for or about the groups.
6. Plan to start new groups regularly.

Do your best to present a strong challenge. Do not waste your time by watering it down and presenting a non-challenge.

Be grateful for anyone who responds. Do not be judgmental about any who do not respond. Do not try to force a decision on anyone.

TO SUNDAY SCHOOL TEACHERS

After interpreting the challenge to a group call for a discussion on one or several Sundays of the challenge period by using any of the following questions:

1. How do you feel about discipline in general?
2. How do you feel about spiritual discipline?
3. Have any of you ever focused on a spiritual discipline by practicing it for a time? Will you tell us about your experience with it?
4. What seems unreasonable about the spiritual discipline we just heard about?
5. What seems reasonable about it?
6. What type of persons do you think will be attracted by this challenge and will want to participate in a group?
7. What type would not be attracted to it?
8. Is the period of thirty days too short to do any good, or is the short time frame a positive point for you?
9. Have any of you heard about anyone who is thinking about, or has decided to participate?
10. We have some of the books here. Let's see how many want to read about the challenge. (Make a list of who takes a book and who wants one, and help keep them circulating.)
11. Do you think we will find ten?
12. Will you be one?

TO THE YOUTH AND WORKERS WITH YOUTH

The Great Experiment is not just an "adult thing." Youth have as much interest and need as anyone to put God first in their lives. Make the challenge a meaningful part of the youth experience in your church.

Circulate the books among the youth so as many as possible will know the full meaning of the challenge.

The youth Great Experiment group should always have competent and committed adult leadership who have participated themselves and have the confidence of the youth.

TO THE CHURCH BOARD
(or other such groups)

During this challenge period do all you can to invite and encourage as many as possible to read the book. As church leaders each of you may have more responsibility than anyone else to invite persons to consider the challenge to put God first. Call forth the best response in all areas of your influence.

But remember, this is a personal challenge, which means that your influence will be needed in two ways:

First, encourage response, but do not push. Do not intimidate. Do not assume. Do not judge others. Some persons will surprise you with their response; others will disappoint you. Be positive, helpful, friendly, and loving, as you talk with people about the challenge. If (and when) you decide to participate, let your decision be known within the circle of your influence.

Second, as a spiritual leader of the church, you have more than official responsibility for leadership. This invitation to put God first is a direct invitation to you, personally. We are hoping to find ten. Will you be one? It is a very personal challenge to you.

All of you are leaders. Your spiritual leadership in presenting this church-wide challenge will be profoundly helpful. Make the challenge a central part of your overall program and business meeting during the challenge period. For some persons, you will be the only leader that has their attention. Do all you can to encourage the people in *your* group to put God first.

Appendix A

FREQUENTLY ASKED QUESTIONS

1. **What is the purpose of the Great Experiment group?** It provides a covenant community that can help guide persons in their desire and commitment to put God first. It is a safe place to experiment with authentic spiritual principles. It is also like a spiritual rocket booster and often launches persons into ministry.

2. **How long should I remain in the group?** For at least a month, for as long as it is meaningful to you and you are growing spiritually, and until you are well on your way to doing what God calls you to do.

3. **How long should the group continue?** For as long as it has life . . . and spirit . . . and passion . . . and power. One group has continued for twenty-two years, another for sixteen years. These are very unusual groups and are not the norm or the goal. Because of their longevity, the people in these groups kept changing. Some dropped out and others joined, but also "the people kept changing" within themselves because of the presence and power of the Holy Spirit and the strength of this covenant commitment and community.

4. **Why are there only four months of Scriptures listed for Great Experiment groups?** The hope is that after four months of reading and applying the Bible as suggested here, the group will have begun to find its own way in the Scriptures. It will be an interesting and formative experience for the group to devise its own plan for getting themselves into the Word.

Appendix B

COMMITMENT FORM

———◆•••◆———

WANTED: Ten Brave Christians Who, For One Month, Will . . .

1. Meet once a week to learn how to pray.
2. Work at least two hours in the church each week and do a daily good deed. (self-surrender)
3. Give God one-tenth of your earnings. (self-denial)
4. Spend from 5:30 to 6:00 each morning in prayer and the study of Scripture. (self-control)
5. Witness about your experience with God to others.

- -

I have read the above carefully and fully understand the implications of giving my life to God during the month of _____.

To prepare my life to receive from God the great strength and power available through prayer, I ask to be a member of this prayer group: _____.
(indicate the time/group you plan to attend)

Signed _____

Mailing Address _____

Telephone No. _____

E-mail Address _____

Please cut on the dotted line and submit form.

Appendix C

SCHEDULE FOR MORNING PRAYER AND SCRIPTURE READING

5:30–5:40

Read scheduled Scripture for the day. Pray and meditate on this Scripture. Write out in fifty words or less how this passage applies to your life.

5:40–5:50

Write out one totally unselfish and unexpected act of kindness or generosity you will do today. Name the person—then act during the day, vigorously and with love and compassion. Keep a written record of (1) the reaction of the person toward whom the kindness is extended and (2) the effect of this act on you personally.

5:50–6:00

Write out carefully how you would like to build and develop your life. Go into great detail if you desire. Take your time—be thoughtful and prayerful. One well prayed-out and thought-out sentence per day would be excellent progress.

IMPORTANT SUGGESTIONS

Let each of your prayers petition God for:
1. A sense of divine direction for your life.
2. An understanding of the need for total surrender to God's will.
3. Great strength of mind for the development of self-discipline.

Appendix D

SCRIPTURE READINGS

FIRST MONTH

The passages for the first month were carefully selected and arranged in a rhythmic pattern. One passage may challenge, the next may affirm, the next may comfort, and the next may arouse. Together, they provide a unique personal invitation to put God first.

Day	Scripture	Day	Scripture	Day	Scripture
1	2 Chron. 7:14	12	Matt. 6:6	23	John 14:27
2	James 4:16	13	Luke 11:9–10	24	Ps. 1:1–3
3	1 John 1:9	14	Isa. 58:9–11	25	John 14:1
4	John 15:6–7	15	Ps. 127:1	26	Matt. 6:25–33
5	Mark 11:24	16	Ps. 66:18	27	Ps. 23:1–6
6	Phil. 4:6	17	Isa. 59:1–3	28	Mark 12:30
7	1 John 5:14	18	Prov. 28:9–10	29	Heb. 12:1
8	Jer. 29:13	19	Matt. 8:24–27	30	John 4:14
9	Matt. 6:7–13	20	John 6:47	31	Matt. 5:13–16
10	Matt. 18:19	21	Eccles. 8:1–8		
11	Isa. 65:23–24	22	Ps. 55:22		

SECOND MONTH

Consider continuing for as long as the group chooses. When a group continues the disciplines for the second month, use the same format for the morning devotional time. The suggested passages for the second month are on mental and spiritual qualities for building a peaceful, powerful, and productive life.

Day	Verse	Qualities	Day	Verse	Qualities
1	John 15:4–7	Abiding in Christ	17	Col. 2:6–7	Gratitude
2	John 14:6	Access to God	18	Rom. 5:5	Hope
3	Heb. 10:22	Assurance	19	Matt. 16:24	Self-Denial
4	John 13:12	Love	20	Heb. 12:1–2	Steadfastness
5	Luke 10:34	Compassion	21	Phil. 4:8	Virtue
6	Exod. 32:39	Consecration	22	1 Cor. 13	Charity
7	Josh. 1:7	Courage	23	Gen. 41:35–36	Frugality
8	Matt. 10:32	Endurance	24	Luke 6:23	Happiness
9	2 Cor. 5:7	Faith	25	1 Cor. 15:58	Perseverance
10	Titus 2:10	Fidelity	26	Luke 9:51	Purpose
11	Eph. 4:32	Forgiveness	27	Prov. 26:16	Reason
12	1 Cor. 15:58	Fortitude	28	Prov. 16:32	Self-control
13	Luke 6:38	Generosity	29	1 Tim. 4:16	Self-respect
14	Acts 20:35	Giving	30	1 Cor. 16:2	Thrift
15	Matt. 7:12	Golden Rule	31	Prov. 8:13	Wisdom
16	Luke 23:50–51	Righteousness			

THIRD MONTH

Scripture selections for the third month are on two of the most basic tenets of the Christian life: love and prayer. Broadly speaking, we may say that love is the essence of *who you are* and prayer is the essence of *what you do*.

LOVE

Day	Scripture	Day	Scripture
1	1 John 4:8	11	Rom. 8:35–39
2	Mark 12:32–34	12	Eph. 3:19
3	1 Tim. 6:10–12	13	John 15:12
4	Prov. 10–12	14	1 John 4:7
5	Matt. 5:46–47	15	Deut. 6:5–7
6	1 John 2:15	16	Mic. 6:8
7	1 John 4:18–21	17	1 John 4:10
8	Rom. 10:13	18	Matt. 22:37–40
9	1 John 5:14–15	19	John 14:15
10	John 15:17	20	John 14:18

PRAYER

Day	Scripture
21	Phil. 4:6
22	Jer. 29:13
23	John 9:31
24	James 5:16
25	1 John 3
26	John 15:6–7
27	Isa. 65:23–24
28	Isa. 58:9
29	Jer. 33:3
30	1 Kings 3:11–14

FOURTH MONTH

The Book of Acts tells of the beginning of the church of Jesus Christ. It tells of the people, the problems, the power, and the promise of the church. The church will become first for the person who puts God first. Acts is not only God's story, and the church's story—it is our story.

ACTS IN THIRTY DAYS

Day	Verse	Subject	Day	Verse	Subject
1	1:1–26	Dear Theophilus	16	14:1–28	In Inconium
2	2:1–47	Coming of the Holy Spirit	17	15:1–35	Meeting at Jerusalem
3	3:1–4:22	The Lame Man Healed	18	15:36–16:10	Paul and Barnabas Separate
4	4:23–37	Believers Pray for Boldness	19	16:11–40	In Philippi: Conversion of Lydia
5	5:1–42	Ananias and Sapphira	20	17:1–34	In Thessalonica
6	6:1–7	The Seven Helpers	21	18:1–23	In Corinth
7	6:8–7:53	Arrest of Stephen	22	18:24–19:20	Apollos in Ephesus and Corinth
8	7:54–60	Stoning of Stephen	23	19:21–20:6	The Riot in Ephesus
9	8:1–40	Saul Persecutes the Church	24	20:7–21:16	Paul's Last Visit in Troas
10	9:1–31	Conversion of Saul	25	21:17–23:11	Paul Visits James
11	9:32–10:33	Peter in Lydda and Joppa	26	23:12–24:27	The Plot Against Paul's Life
12	10:34–48	Peter's Speech	27	25:1–26:32	Paul Appeals to the Emperor
13	11:1–30	Peter's Report to the Church at Jerusalem	28	27:1–44	Paul Sails for Rome
14	12:1–25	More Persecution	29	28:1–15	In Malta
15	13:1–52	Barnabas and Saul Chosen and Sent	30	28:16–31	In Rome